W9-BZV-379

DATE			
NA	CHP		
MAR 2 1	MR 3 0 06		
CPM APR 0 2			
cha MR 18 '04			
upy			
JE 03 05			
upy			
FE 2 8 06			

Gone Again
Ptarmigan

By Jonathan London

Illustrated by Jon Van Zyle

NATIONAL GEOGRAPHIC SOCIETY

Washington, D.C.

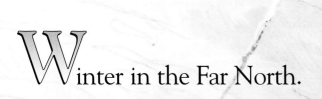

Winter in the Far North.

At the edge of the woods
a lynx pads softly
on big, furry paws
across the snow.

A snowshoe hare
hops, then stops,
in a bowl
of white.
Lynx crouches
then creeps silently, slowly…

and *pounces!*

The snow explodes. *Ptarmigan!*

They circle up and away.
Then settle again—the color of winter.

Gone again ptarmigan.

A ptarmigan's foot
acts like a snowshoe.

A snowy owl—
eyes huge yellow moons—
glides silent as mist
over the open valley.

Below, in feathers of
purest snowy white,
the ptarmigan huddle.
Does the big owl spot them?

Great Snowy
dive-bombs down,
claws extended...

and nabs a lemming instead.

Gone again ptarmigan.

A lemming crouches in the snow.

Spring creeps slowly
across the land. Snow melts
into bogs and pools.
Feathers darkening,
the ptarmigan wing north
and land among dwarf willow and spruce.

A short-tailed weasel,
hungry after the long winter, watches.
But behind it
a gray shadow stalks.

Leaves in the snow

Wolverine.

In a flurry of fur
Wolverine chases Weasel,
and the ptarmigan disappear
into splotches of snow
and muddy, brown earth.

Gone again ptarmigan.

Summer finds eggs
cradled in a bowl
of grass and leaves.
Mama Ptarmigan broods
while Papa Ptarmigan
keeps watch,
blending with the thick brush.

*Ptarmigan eggs are just
waiting to hatch.*

Soon, eggs crack open
and downy chicks struggle free.
Hours later they toddle after Mama,
exploring hillsides for spiders,
crowberries, and flowers—
early harebells, and forget-me-nots.

From around a hill
a huge grizzly stumbles upon them.
Mama and the chicks hold as still
as the stones that surround them.

A brand-new ptarmigan chick

Papa shouts:
Go back! Go back! Go back!
and flails at the startled grizzly
as the ptarmigan family flees.

Having molted—from winter white
to summer brown—they settle down,
disguised as a jumble
of barren rocks.

Gone again ptarmigan.

Ptarmigan nestle in the rocks.

In September, a red fox trots
among autumn colors.
Matching fallen leaves,
the ptarmigan nip
at the last of the blueberries.

Flame colored in the low sun,
Fox *pounces…*

Field mouse

and pins a mouse instead.

The ptarmigan flare and land
among the fallen leaves.

Gone again ptarmigan.

As winter blasts in from the north,
the ptarmigan sail farther south,
their feathers again changing
to the color of snow.

By the end of the year,
near a frozen river
in a sheltered valley,
the flock scratches deep
for willow twigs and spruce needles.

Snowflake

It is night.
It is almost always night now.
A wolf shape ghosts
among the gnarled black spruce,
closer, and closer yet.

Suddenly there's a roar
of wind from the mountains,
and a raging blizzard swirls,
turning the night white.

A wolf paw print in the snow

When all clears, Gray Wolf's howl
drifts across the forest,
and the northern lights blaze
above the white world.

And the ptarmigan snuggle down
in the deep drifts.

Gone again ptarmigan.

The willow ptarmigan (TAR-me-gan)—otherwise known as snow grouse, willow grouse, Arctic grouse, or willow partridge—is a very special bird. In fact, in a vote taken by Alaska schoolchildren, the willow ptarmigan was selected as the official state bird.

Ptarmigan range across Alaska and Canada and, at high elevations, live as far south as New Mexico. The willow ptarmigan of this story (the other species are rock ptarmigan and white-tailed ptarmigan) live along the top of the world, in Arctic and alpine regions of North America and

Eurasia. How do these beautiful birds survive in a land of such bitter cold and danger? Like some other Arctic animals, they survive by camouflage. Willow ptarmigan are masters of disguise, famous for their "disappearing act." White in winter, mottled in varying shades of white and brown in spring and fall and summer, they blend in to the landscape and thus escape a predator's eyes. Arctic foxes, short-tailed weasels (known as ermine in their winter coats), and snowshoe hares are some of the other Arctic animals whose coats change with the seasons. Many non-Arctic creatures also depend upon camouflage. Perhaps best known is the chameleon, which has the ability to change the color of its skin.

Besides camouflage, willow ptarmigan have another feature that helps assure their survival. Full-feathered feet and toes insulate them from the tremendous cold—down to -80°F (-62°C). In winter these feet are "feathered snowshoes."

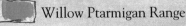

Willow Ptarmigan Range

(The generic name for ptarmigan in Latin is *Lagopus,* which means "rabbit-footed.") With these feathered snowshoes, ptarmigan can hop about in deep snow without sinking in.

Ptarmigan couples mate in May and stay together for life. The female lays 7 to 12 eggs, which hatch after incubating for 22 days. Only the mother sits on the eggs, but the willow ptarmigan father stays close and helps protect the nest. Though ptarmigan rely on camouflage, if a predator comes upon them, the father may fly at it, flailing and cackling loudly, or the mother may act as if she has a broken wing and try to lure the predator away.

Within one hour of hatching, chicks can leave the nest and start learning to peck and nip at buds and bugs, twigs and berries—the same food the adults eat. Chicks make their first short jumping flights when they are one week old. For 60 days, until the young can be on their own, both parents help care for them. If the mother is killed, the father will take over care of the family.

Willow ptarmigan are migratory. In winter they gather in flocks and fly south hundreds of miles to sheltered valleys, then back north as the summer months approach. Wherever they settle down in ptarmigan country—whether it's a jumble of barren rocks, tundra brush, or drifts of blowing snow—they blend with the landscape and disappear: Gone again ptarmigan.

*A ptarmigan feather and
blueberries in autumn*

*For Jon Van Zyle, who asked
for it, and for the schoolchildren
of Alaska — JL*

*For Jona, for your inspiration
— JVZ*

*To create his paintings, Jon Van Zyle used acrylics on masonite panels.
His field sketches are acrylics on Strathmore cold-pressed watercolor paper.*

The text of this book is set in Goudy.

Book design by Dorrit Green and Jon Van Zyle

Printed in Mexico

The world's largest nonprofit scientific and educational organization, the National Geographic
Society was founded in 1888 "for the increase and diffusion of geographic knowledge." Since
then it has supported scientific exploration and spread information to its more than nine million
members worldwide.

The National Geographic Society educates and inspires millions every day through magazines,
books, television programs, videos, maps and atlases, research grants, the National Geographic
Bee, teacher workshops, and innovative classroom materials.

The Society is supported through membership dues and income from the sale of its educational products. Members receive
NATIONAL GEOGRAPHIC magazine—the Society's official journal—discounts on Society products, and other benefits.

For more information about the National Geographic Society and its educational programs and publications,
please call 1-800-NGS-LINE (647-5463), or write to the following address:

National Geographic Society
1145 17th Street N.W.
Washington, D.C. 20036-4688 U.S.A.

Visit the Society's Web site: www.nationalgeographic.com